# Builders Under Fire

## How Builders Operate When Systems Are Overwhelmed

**Jamil Hasan**

First Edition · 2026
Published by Crypto Hipster Publications

ISBN: 978-1-972991-08-4

Cover design by Jamil Hasan
Interior design by Jamil Hasan



Printed in the United States of America

For Team Quasar—without your support, I wouldn't
be the man I am today

Builders Under Fire

Systems don't fail all at once.
They fail when the conditions they depend on no longer hold.

Stability is often mistaken for resilience.
Repetition creates confidence, but it does not prove durability.

Most systems are never tested outside the environment for which they were built.
They appear reliable because the conditions remain stable.

When those conditions shift, the system gradually decreases.

It becomes unavailable when it is needed most.

What matters at that moment is not the design.
It is not the intention.

It is whether anything can still be used.

Builders don't operate in theory.
They operate at the point where systems stop working as expected.

They adapt.

They reroute.
They use what remains.

This book is about what happens next.

Not how systems are designed—but how they
behave when conditions overwhelm them.

And what builders do when the structure they had
relied on is no longer there.

# Preface

I'm Jamil Hasan. People call me the Crypto Hipster—a name I gave myself, and one I've chosen to own. It started as a joke. A meme. Then it became a signal. Not rebellion for its own sake, but a way of seeing things.

Crypto moves quickly—often faster than understanding can keep up. Sometimes, a topic I spent several podcast episodes fully understanding in one week completely changed the next.

There is a tremendous amount of noise in the market and not enough uncovering of the true signal. I aim to change that.

Discussion about the price of Bitcoin, meme-coin hype, 1000x speculation, and repeated narratives never truly interested me. I wanted to find out what actually matters.

So I started the Crypto Hipster Podcast in February 2021. Not to chase headlines, but to have genuine conversations with people building in this space.

Founders. Creators. Thinkers. People who are trying to reshape systems.

Crypto Hipster became more than a podcast. Nine seasons. Over 580 conversations. Hundreds of written works.

Then I hit an uncomfortable truth:

Curating discussions is not the same as creating ideas.

For years, I documented conversations. Published transcripts. Built an archive. A colleague told me that if I wanted to be an influential voice, I would have to do more than host conversations—I would have to move them forward.

That person was right.

This book is the fourth of sixty-seven Crypto Hipster Curtain Calls compilations spanning 281 interviewees. It marks the beginning of that shift.

Curtain Calls differs from my first 399 books. It is not a collection of transcripts. It is an interpretive synthesis of conversations, ideas, and lived experiences. It is where my voice meets the voices of the people I've learned from.

Crypto is not just technology. It is about power. About identity. About freedom. And above all, about people.

My path into this space came not from comfort. For the past five years, I have fought an aggressive desmoid tumor. What occupied my mind became something more. It became a way to process the world—and my place in it.

This book blends two things:

The conversations I've had with builders of the
digital economy
The lessons I have lived myself

Conversations and memoirs woven together.

You will see both here. Ideas about decentralization
and finance. About infrastructure and governance.

You will also see stories. Resilience. Failure. Faith.
Relationships. Recovery.

This technology does not exist in isolation. It
reflects who we are.

Too often, crypto is reduced to price charts. The
authentic story runs deeper:

Whether these systems actually change anything—
or simply recreate old structures with new labels

Whether innovation leads to freedom—or just a
novel form of control
Whether we choose to participate intentionally—or
drift with the current

This book is my attempt to slow that down. To take
hundreds of conversations and extract what
matters.

To connect patterns.

To ask better questions.

To share what I've learned—not as answers, but as a
framework for thinking.

This is not just my story.

It's an invitation.

An invitation to think differently. To question more.
To build with intention.

And if you see yourself in these pages, I hope this book inspires you to write your own story—with more clarity, purpose, and conviction.

# Table of Contents


**The Illusion of Stability**      1
**The Conditions Before Pressure**      15

**Identity Under Pressure**      33
**The First Break**      47
**What Holds / What Adapts**      63
**What Emerges**      81

**Old Paradigms Die Hard**      97

**About the Author**      115
**Crypto Hipster Conversations**      117

# The Illusion of Stability

The first time I realized systems don't hold just because they exist wasn't a dramatic failure. It was a slow realization. Things that looked stable were conditional. The structures I trusted were not built to handle the kinds of pressure they later faced.

The actual logic of a system reveals itself in how it behaves under pressure. Not in the plan. Not in the intent. In what happens.

I worked inside places that looked stable. Size made them seem durable, and rules and institutions made them seem official. I picked up the habit of assuming continuity—processes had worked before, so they would work again. They would kick in when needed. I never tested them under pressure.

Normal conditions had been enough to convince everyone. Repetition fed belief, and belief fed reliance. Meanwhile, no one checked the conditions that made that repetition possible.

From inside a system, you miss something obvious: consistency is not resilience. A process that gives the same result every day can still break when conditions change. The first signs are subtle—small deviations, a response that doesn't fully show up, a process that runs but doesn't deliver what you expected. People explain it away or delay digging into it. The system still looks like it works.

One moment is simple to ignore. Enough of them form a pattern, showing the system runs under a narrower set of conditions than assumed. Its apparent stability depends on variables you can't always see. When those variables shift, the system won't adapt fast enough. It falls out of alignment.

At AIG, scale and complexity made that danger feel less real. Size felt like durability. Complexity felt like control. Both created the expectation that pressure would be spread out and failure wouldn't reach the surface. But systems don't absorb pressure forever. They move it around, and it finds concentration points.

When those points hit a threshold, the system doesn't fade. It breaks at the moment people expect it to hold the most. When that happens, the consequences are severe.

This realization didn't flip a switch from stability to collapse. It changed how I saw things. The belief that a system will keep going just because it exists was replaced by the understanding that its function is conditional. And that applies to any system that runs on assumptions instead of verified behavior. After that, you stop assuming systems will hold and start asking how they behave when their assumptions aren't true.

That shift is sharper when you build inside systems instead of just working within them. The gap between what you can see and what actually matters becomes obvious. The visible layer is not always what decides the outcome.

When I started building my media content business, the focus wasn't really on the content. It was on distribution—what actually gets content to users. Making content became easy. Getting it to people didn't. Distribution depended on access, relationships, and infrastructure you couldn't always see.

From the outside, that work doesn't look like execution. There's no immediate revenue stream, so people call it delay or inaction. But it's the layer that decides whether anything else works. No distribution, no audience. No pathway, no system. It can look finished on the surface and still be useless.

This difference between what you see and what makes things work matters when systems are tested under pressure. The parts that seem important are not always the parts that hold. The parts that hold are not always the parts that were central. So you have to look past the visible structure and see how dependencies interact when conditions change.

I learned that in a more painful way when I lost 400,000 UBT tokens. Not in theory. As a direct hit. It showed how systems can be navigated and exploited when you misunderstand the assumptions they run on. The safeguards worked as designed, but the outcome was still a failure. The system wasn't broken in a broad sense. The way I interacted with it didn't match the expectations behind its use.

This draws a logical line between design and behavior. A system can follow its internal rules exactly and still produce an outcome the user didn't intend. Once you feel that misalignment, you can't pretend the structure guarantees reliability anymore. You need a different approach.

Understand before you assume. Evaluate rather than just trust.

After that, systems stopped feeling neutral. They stopped being fixed backgrounds for action. They became dynamic—things to assess all the time, especially how they react to pressure. The moments you rely on them most are often the moments they're least predictable.

That view shaped every conversation afterward. Not asking what a system claims to do, but how it behaves when pushed beyond its design. That's what set the builders in Ukraine apart. They didn't talk about systems in theory. They talked about systems about to be tested. Their assumptions were about to be checked. Design would meet reality. The intent would meet the use. The gap between them would be impossible to ignore.

You learn that failure isn't where it first appears. The visible breakdown is usually the end of a chain of dependencies that had already drifted. What looks like a single event is the point where accumulated misalignment can't be hidden. That moment reveals the system's limits—and the assumptions behind them.

That's how systems can look steady for a long time while hiding fragility. As long as the conditions they need stay within a certain range, they act consistently. That consistency breeds confidence. But that confidence hasn't been tested against what lies outside that range. It's a kind of stability that's real in a narrow context and unreliable beyond it. So failure isn't just something not working. It's the exposure of how narrow the system's operating range actually is—and how that range depends on variables you might not see.

That's why the shift from steady to broken often feels sudden, even though the causes were building. The system wasn't asked to show its limits until it had already been pushed past them.

Once you've lived through that pattern, the signs mean more. Minor glitches. Odd delays. Inconsistent results. Things you used to call anomalies become warning signals. They point to a system running closer to its limits than anyone realized. They suggest it may not absorb more pressure.

What makes acting on this hard is that systems are usually judged on normal days. You measure performance in comfort, not under pressure. So there's a gap between how they're measured and how they behave when it counts. That gap makes people trust steady performance over real resilience. But resilience decides whether the system holds.

This is not just about big institutions. The same thing happens in small systems, processes, and any interaction that seems stable until the supporting conditions change. Then the limits show up in ways you couldn't fully predict, because some variables only appear under pressure.

Losing those 400,000 UBT made that plain. It showed a system doing what it was built to do and still producing a result that didn't match what the user expected. Knowing the mechanics of a system is not the same as knowing how it will behave in every situation—especially when the situation involves interactions the design didn't fully cover.

That's when the idea of control wobbles. What looks like control from the outside relies on unchallenged conditions. Change those conditions, and the sense of control vanishes fast. You see what the system enforces, and how much of its stability depended on things that were never actively managed. This doesn't mean systems are useless. They still matter. They still create value. But it changes how you treat them—from assumption to testing, from passive reliance to active work, from trusting structure to trusting observed behavior, especially under pressure.

Seeing things this way makes patterns visible across very different systems. The logic is the same whether the system is financial, technical, or organizational. It becomes visible when the system is pushed outside the conditions for which it was designed. Then you see priorities, responses, and points of failure. It also changes how you assess new systems. You stop just looking at the intended function. You look at dependencies, likely failure points, and how the system behaves if those dependencies disappear.

Often, the systems that seem less complete in calm times perform better under pressure if they don't rely on the same broken assumptions. That lens followed me into conversations with builders—not as a rule I imposed, but to hear what they were saying. We didn't just judge current functionality. We asked how these systems would behave when pressure finds them. That's where design and reality stop agreeing.

In Ukraine, that pressure wasn't theoretical. The systems were close to facing it. So, the questions weren't about isolated performance. They were about usable performance when conditions change. Could these systems work without assumptions that might not hold? Could they keep operating when the environment became unpredictable?

That made the conversations different. They weren't academic. They were real. These systems were close to moments of validation. Design would be tested by reality. What people intended would run up against what could actually be used. That's where this book starts. Not with systems themselves, but with the idea that systems are only as reliable as the conditions they depend on.

Once those conditions change, the only question is what, if anything, can still be used. What this ultimately reframes is not just how systems fail, but how we trust them.

Trust that grows from repetition instead of real validation sticks. It stays until something forces it to face conditions for which it was never meant. When that happens, the change is not small. It comes fast. The assumptions that once felt solid fall away. You see that stability was always conditional, tied to things you did not always see or control.

Think about operating within tight constraints. Rules meant to create stability end up changing how people act—not in ways you expected. Fix one risk and you usually create another. You move the pressure around instead of removing it.

The results make sense to the system but not to the people inside it. Design intent and experienced impact don't always match. The effect is often quiet. It does not always look like failure. People adjust, find other routes, and change what they expect.

They keep the work going even when the system no longer fits their needs. A parallel layer of behavior grows alongside the formal structure. It doesn't replace it. It fills the gaps.

You notice the pattern once you've seen it enough times. It shows that systems are not fixed—they change, shaped as much by how they are used as by how they are built.

The actual test of a system is not how it runs in calm times.

It is how it behaves when conditions shift, when assumptions fail, when the only question left is whether anything at all can still be used.

Systems do not hold because they exist. They hold only as long as the conditions that support them remain. Once those conditions shift, what looked stable becomes something else entirely. The question is not whether a system exists, but whether it still fits the world it operates within.

# The Conditions Before Pressure

What makes systems hard to judge before they are tested is that people usually evaluate them under the conditions they were built. They seem to do what they're supposed to do. That builds a kind of confidence that makes sense inside the system but isn't proven outside it.

The system looks sound because it produces expected output. But often the range of conditions you've seen is smaller than you think. Only when those conditions shift do the limits show.

Ukraine, before the war, sat in that space. Not fragile, but actively modernizing. Building infrastructure that cut friction and made things more accessible. Moving toward digitization. The way people and the state interacted was changing. Systems were faster, easier to use, and more direct. It looked like progress—not just better features, but a unique structure.

The idea of a "State in a Smartphone" wasn't framed as a reaction to pressure. It felt like the next step in how systems work when things are stable. Identity, documents, and services were all available without the old delays and dependencies. People could deal with the state more directly, with fewer sticking points.

That made it appear that the system was aligning with what users needed. Sergey Vasylchuk put it plainly: the plan was to have "trust built into the smartphone." What you sign there would carry the same legal weight as traditional methods. Seen on its own, that shift looks small and incremental. But it's a larger change in how identity and authority are handled.

Moving from physical checks to digital validation makes processes faster and reduces reliance on central systems. But this shift didn't happen in isolation. It was part of a broader environment—

technical capability, economic incentives, and cultural familiarity with systems all played a role.

In Ukraine, technical education, software development, and system-level thinking were widespread. People could use these tools not as theory, but as something practical. That mix of infrastructure and know-how made the system seem forward-looking. The fit extended beyond any one country.

Digitizing services, cutting friction, and moving to direct interaction—these were treated as signs of progress. That strengthened the belief that these systems would be resilient and adaptable. And yet the assumptions behind that belief hadn't been fully tested. The system hadn't been pushed into the conditions that reveal whether those assumptions hold.

Judging it by normal performance left open the question of how it would work under different conditions. Builders understood parts of this. But they weren't focused on stress-testing the system against extreme cases. They worked on improving it—adding features and matching user needs. That's how most systems grow. Incremental improvement, not confrontation with the conditions that will define their limits.

Conversations with builders from that time don't give a sense of imminent collapse. They give a sense of possibility. They focus on what the systems enable, not on the ways they could fail. Accessibility. Efficiency. Innovation. The default belief: the system will keep working in the conditions that make those things matter.

Andrej Šimunaj, part of White Rabbit, framed it that way—focusing on access, usability, and minimal friction operation. That shows the system was being evaluated under conditions that still supported its assumptions, not the ones that would test them.

Still, there were quieter signals of a more complex picture. Not loud warnings. More like tensions you see if you think about how systems behave under pressure. Reliance on centralized components. Dependence on legal recognition. Assumptions about infrastructure availability. These are the places that become constraints when conditions change.

This isn't only about Ukraine or government systems. Any system tuned for efficiency in a fixed environment carries the same risk. Optimization reduces flexibility. If you tune a system for one set of conditions, it struggles when those conditions change—especially if adaptation isn't built into the design. The wider world reinforced that dynamic.

Global finance and tech were operating under conditions that hadn't been tested. New mechanisms expanded. Digital assets grew. Interconnected systems became more complex. It looked like innovation. It looked like progress. But it also introduced dependencies that weren't visible on the surface.

The FTX collapse later exposed many of those dependencies. It matters not because it directly changed Ukraine's systems, but because it shows how stability can break when assumptions fail. Performance in normal times doesn't predict behavior under pressure.

Looking back, the builders' conversations take on a different meaning. They capture when systems were expanding without being forced to confront the conditions that would define them. They show intent—and the assumptions built in before those assumptions were tested.

The systems weren't broken. They were unvalidated across the full range of possibilities. Any untested system is like that. Validation requires exposure to conditions that reveal how a system performs, how it fails, and how it adapts after failure.

The key moment is not what the systems were, but what they were about to become. The move from stability to pressure is where design and reality diverge—where systems that looked fine have to show whether they can keep working when the environment changes in ways not fully expected. What follows is not more of the same. It's a shift into a new phase of behavior.

The conditions that once supported function are replaced by ones that challenge it. Adapting becomes more important than performing in ideal circumstances. Because what was being built then was not only infrastructure. It was expectation. And once expectation exists, it becomes the baseline people use to judge the system when it's tested.

So, the move into pressure is technical and perceptual. The gap between what was assumed and what is experienced gets hard to ignore. And it is in that gap that the next chapter begins.

What makes developing these systems so striking is not just that they cut friction or make things easier to access. It's that they change how trust actually works. When identity, documents, and permissions move into a digital space, the system stops leaning on physical checks or institutions in the same way. It relies on its own internal logic.

That logic must be precise enough to carry legal and social weight without the old processes backing it up. From inside a stable setup, this shift looks small. Things still feel the same. People can access services, prove who they are, and deal with institutions, noticing nothing radical. But underneath, the structure is different. The point of trust has moved—from the institution to the mechanism, from the authority that verifies to the system that executes.

So the dependency becomes less visible but more concentrated. As Vasylchuk explains, the expectation is that "when we can sign something inside a smartphone, what we sign is legally our signature." It collapses action and validation into a single moment. No extra layers of confirmation.

The system can move faster because it no longer waits on external checks. But that compression creates a different dependency. It removes friction for users—and increases reliance on internal consistency.

The system's integrity becomes critical to both function and legitimacy. If that integrity breaks—technically, legally, or in the infrastructure—every dependent interaction is affected. This is where the idea of a "State in a Smartphone" stops being convenient. It becomes a concentration. Identity, access, and interaction collapse into a single interface.

That interface must work across a wide range of conditions. Many of those conditions are assumed, not tested—especially what happens when the underlying infrastructure is disrupted. The upside is clear in stable environments. Faster. Less friction. More access. It feels efficient. It feels aligned. But the question remains: how does that concentration behave when assumptions fail? When connectivity drops, when access becomes uneven, when new variables appear that the system never accounted for?

This isn't just about digital identity. It applies to any system designed for speed. Consolidation removes redundancy. Redundancy looks wasteful in stable conditions. But under pressure, redundancy creates options. So systems that optimize for speed and simplicity also need to account for how those choices become constraints when conditions change.

What you could see in Ukraine before the war was a system pushing toward more efficiency, more access, and more digital capability. What you couldn't see was how that system would react when those capabilities were tested—when people needed not just speed but resilience, not just access but adaptability, not just function but continuity through disruption.

That's why design and validation matter. A system can be cleanly designed for its intended use and still never be tested in ways that matter. Lack of testing doesn't prove weakness. But it leaves open the question of how the system behaves outside its parameters. That is where you find its genuine character.

This moment matters not only for what's being built, but for the environment shaping it. In Ukraine, these systems grow inside a broader context where technical capability, economic incentives, and global system dynamics are converging. That creates opportunity and latent tension at the same time. Progress is visible. Dependencies sit just below the surface. Builders aren't outside these forces. They engage with them.

They draw on global systems, integrate new technologies, and shape a fast-moving landscape.

Local and global systems blur together. One system's behavior can affect another in ways you don't always predict. Conversations with builders from this period show a steady focus on what the systems enable—how they cut friction, widen access, and open new ways to interact. There is less focus on how things might break. That's not ignorance. It reflects the environment.

Conditions do not yet force that kind of scrutiny. The emphasis stays on building, not stress-testing. There are hints, though, that these systems assume continuity. Infrastructure will be there. Coordination will work. The environment will support operations. Those assumptions make sense in context. But they also create fragility when you look at how systems behave under pressure.

These conversations carry two meanings. They are rooted in the present. And they gain weight when viewed later. Statements about efficiency or scalability can be read again as questions about how those traits hold up when the supporting conditions vanish. You see both strengths and limitations.

Global events like the FTX collapse underline this. Not because they affected Ukraine directly, but because they show how quickly confidence can shift when a system's assumptions are exposed. That stability depends on conditions you don't always see. And perceived reliability can change quickly when those things break.

That creates a moment where local development and global behavior align. Patterns in one place help you understand another, even when the details differ. Systems across domains face the same dynamics when pushed outside their design environments.

The builders aren't described as expecting this shift. Yet their work is moving toward it. The systems they create become more capable, more integrated, and more dependent on conditions that haven't been challenged. Their effectiveness is understood within a certain range—but not beyond it.

That's where the tension comes from. Nothing has failed. Everything appears to work. Still, the conditions that will define these systems are forming beneath the surface—not as shocks, but as pressures that will push them beyond their assumptions. What's being built is not just function. It's expectation. And once expectation exists, it becomes the standard by which the system is judged when it's tested.

The shift in pressure changes perception. The gap between what was assumed and what people experience becomes how the system is understood. It is in that shift that the next phase begins.

Systems built for stability must face instability. The difference between design intent and real capability becomes the central question driving what happens next. What makes this moment feel different isn't just that systems are becoming more efficient and easier to use. It's that expectations are settling in. When systems keep working the same way in a steady environment, people grow more confident. They assume that those results will continue.

That confidence stretches beyond what has actually been tested. It creates a sense of resilience. But that sense hasn't been checked against conditions outside that steady environment. The match between how a system is designed and what users expect becomes critical.

When a system keeps producing the outcomes people want, it trains them to expect it. That expectation is built on a narrow set of circumstances. When those circumstances shift, the gap between what people expect and what the system delivers can appear quickly—not because the system suddenly changed, but because it's being used in ways it wasn't designed to handle. The system is judged by tests it has never faced.

The people building these systems mostly work on what they can see. They improve features and smooth out frustrations. They open the system to more people. That's how progress happens while conditions remain steady.

The assumptions that allow this are rarely challenged—not because builders ignore them, but because there is no need to test them yet. So the system becomes coherent on the inside but unproven on the outside. You end up with progress and fragility at once. The system improves while becoming more dependent on the conditions that allow it to function.

What looks strong in a calm setting may not hold up under pressure. The actual test is how the system behaves when that alignment breaks.

What sustains a system is rarely visible when it is working. Dependencies hide inside normal conditions. When those conditions change, the system does not adapt immediately. It reveals what it was actually built on—and how little of that was understood.

# Identity Under Pressure

Identity is easy when nothing pushes against it. It lives as a quiet agreement between institutions and people—issued, verified, stored somewhere far away. Most people never have to ask if it will still be there tomorrow, or if the system that recognizes it will keep working.

Because no one asks, identity feels stable. That stability is conditional. I thought the same. I assumed systems would hold because they always had—until I saw how fast that assumption falls apart when the structure stops matching reality.

Ukraine did not start under pressure. It started by trying to remove friction. To make the state immediate and usable. To shorten the distance between a person and the systems that recognize them. Identity would not sit in offices or files. It would move with the person—executable in real time on a device people already carry. A driver's license, a passport, a registration, a signature. No physical presence. No institutional mediation. Produce it, verify it, accept it at the moment.

In calm times, that idea looks like an optimization. Under pressure, it looks more like survival infrastructure. Vasylchuk put it plainly. The goal was not symbolic but structural: "interaction with the government should include trust built into the smartphone," he said. And more importantly, what is signed there "is legally our signature."

That sounds incremental until it is tested. Because this change is not about the interface. It changes where control sits. Identity moves from something institutions grant to something the individual can execute—without delay, without mediation, without waiting for the system to respond.

Even before the system needed to prove itself, its edges were visible. Not as outright failures, but as warnings. Compressing the state to remove friction also concentrates risk. Questions surface. Data exposure. Centralized control points. Can legal recognition keep up with technology? Do users understand what they are now responsible for?

It's easy to postpone those concerns when things are steady. They become immediate when conditions change faster than the system can adapt. From the outside, this phase looks incomplete—the same way building distribution once looked like inaction, long before the product appeared. Systems are rarely validated when they are built. They are validated when they are forced to run in situations they were not designed to run in. That is when the gap between design and reality becomes obvious.

When the war began, that gap collapsed into one question: can identity still work when its basic assumptions no longer hold? For people with access, the answer was immediate. Not because the system was perfect, but because it was usable. A smartphone could present what once required institutional mediation. That presentation could be accepted as valid—not a workaround, but a legally recognized form of identity. Efficiency turned into infrastructure. Vasylchuk's words remove abstraction from the shift. He said that if stopped, he would show documents on his phone "as my legal identity." He described it as "like the government's smartphone, but for everyone."

What he described is not convenience. It is immediacy. Not only is access granted, but access is executed when it is needed. That is the only identity that survives under pressure. Identity does not live only in the systems that issue it; it also lives in systems that can take it away, restrict it, or redefine it.

Long before the war, this second layer was exposed. Not everywhere, but often enough to reveal structural dependency. Banks can freeze accounts. Institutions can block participation. Access can be withdrawn without warning. Identity becomes conditional. It exists only as long as the system recognizing it continues to work for the person.

Marie Poteriaieva put it bluntly: "You never know when things can go south," she said. Or when "the bank will shut down your account." That unpredictability is not a rare glitch. It is a property of centralized systems under changing conditions.

So the idea of removing "obligatory trust" is practical, not ideological. It targets the point when the system stops acting in the person's interest. People building alternatives understand their limitations. As Marie notes, "blockchain is cool, but it is not magic." That honesty matters. It prevents trading one blind assumption for another. What changes is not the removal of risk, but its distribution—moving reliance away from a single point of failure and into systems that can keep working even when parts are under pressure.

You can see that redistribution in how people manage identity under pressure. They do not pick one system and stick to it. They move between them. Use the state system when it is recognized and available. Use decentralized systems when institutional access is blocked. Mix both when needed. That creates a layered identity. Not defined by one authority, but by the ability to maintain access across different contexts.

In Ukraine, this layering was not theoretical. The population had the technical foundation to use it. Engineering, math, and systems thinking are practical skills there, not abstract ones. Identity systems were not treated as black boxes. People understood the tools well enough to trust them conditionally and to use them when needed.

That understanding changes the outcome. Systems people do not understand cannot be used under pressure. Systems that cannot be used may as well not exist. The effectiveness of identity depends not just on infrastructure, but on how people relate to it.

What emerges from this mix is a shift in how identity is defined. Away from documents and toward access. Under pressure, identity reduces to one function: can you still act? Which system works can change in the moment?

For some, that continuity came from digital identity systems that kept working while physical systems wavered. For others, it came from decentralized systems that allowed value and access to persist independently. For many, it meant juggling both—choosing what still worked rather than relying on what was supposed to.

None of it was seamless. Uncertainty remained. But continuity appeared where there might have been none. That continuity determines whether identity holds under pressure. Not the absence of failure, but the ability to keep functioning despite it.

Ukraine did not aim to prove any theory. I did not set out to test systems either when I worked inside them. I assumed they would behave as expected because they always had. Pressure reveals what design cannot. It shows where control really sits, where access really comes from, and whether the system can still be used when ideal conditions are gone.

Identity, like any important system, is defined not by how it performs when everything works, but by whether it keeps working when everything is not working. Under pressure, what survives is not what was efficient. It is what was built to be used.

That distinction only appears once the system stops being theoretical and failure has real consequences. What becomes visible then are the assumptions behind the system. Do they hold when the environment changes faster than the system can respond?

Identity, stripped to its function, is not a static attribute. It is a dynamic interaction between recognition and acceptance—between what is presented and what is validated. Under pressure, that interaction becomes fragile in ways people rarely consider in calm times.

Systems seem reliable until they're pushed outside their conditions. The traditional model assumes continuity: that the institution verifying identity will still be there, that the database will be accessible, and that the authority will remain legitimate.

Those assumptions are layered and interdependent. When one fails, the others do not compensate. They cascade. Gaps appear—where identity works in one context but not in another, where it is technically valid but practically unusable, where the system exists but the person cannot access it when it matters.

That failure mode remains invisible until the system faces actual conditions. Therefore, possession is not the same as usability.

The identity you cannot present is the same as an identity that does not exist. Systems that rely on delayed verification, physical presence, or institutional mediation introduce latency that becomes failure under pressure—not because they are wrong in design, but because they assume time, stability, and cooperation from the environment.

Those assumptions collapse under pressure, as I learned when systems stopped behaving as expected. Digitizing identity aimed to remove that latency—to close the gap between a person and the system, to let identity be produced and verified in the same moment. But collapsing distance does not remove dependence. It shifts from physical to digital infrastructure, from human checks to system checks, from institutional presence to system availability.

Each introduces its own failure modes under pressure. That is why Vasylchuk insisted a digital signature is not symbolic but legally binding. Without that equivalence, the system cannot work under pressure. It can only assist in normal times. Diia was more than a tool. It attempted to realign dependencies so a person could operate identity directly, without waiting for an intermediary. That realignment allowed it to function where traditional systems would have caused delays. The system did not need permission to verify identity. It was built to do it at the point of interaction. Trust was embedded as a function of execution, not an assumption.

That is the practical shift Vasylchuk described. The decentralized layer offers a different model. It does not depend on institutional recognition in the same way. It relies on cryptographic verification and network consensus. It removes some dependencies and introduces others. It cuts the need for a central authority to confirm identity. But it still depends on network availability, user skill, and translating verification into real-world acceptance.

Marie's point that blockchain can remove "obligatory trust" matters only when paired with "blockchain is not magic." What changes is the location of control over uncertainty. You see this redistribution under pressure in behavior, not in theory.

People choose systems based on what still works— switching from state-recognized identity to decentralized systems when needed. Not ideology. Practicality.

Under pressure, choices are about usability. Usability is whether the system grants access when needed. That creates a layered identity environment. Different systems provide different access. People navigate between them—using the state system when it is recognized, decentralized systems when they are independent.

They combine both when necessary. Redundancy emerges—not as a design goal, but because no single system covers all failure modes. Under pressure, continuity comes from the ability to move between systems, not from faith in any of them.

In Ukraine, this layering held not because it was perfect, but because people understood it. The population had the technical literacy to use it without hesitation—to know what a digital signature means, to grasp cryptographic verification, to accept conditional trust instead of absolute trust. That is why it worked under pressure. It did not ask for blind faith. It asked for informed use.

That difference matters. Systems people do not understand cannot be used in a crisis. Systems that cannot be used are effectively dead, no matter how well they were designed. Identity under pressure depends on the relationship between infrastructure and its users. That relationship determines whether identity can keep functioning when the environment moves faster than the system was built for.

What Ukraine shows is not that one system can solve identity in a crisis. It shows that a mix of systems, aligned with the people who use them, can provide continuity that would otherwise be impossible. That continuity is not seamless or universal. It is uneven, conditional, and shifting. But it exists. And in situations of pressure, existence is the only metric that matters. Because when you strip identity of abstractions, it is not about paperwork or even verification. It is about the ability to act. To move. To prove. To participate.

Under pressure, that ability is the only measure that remains. Identity is not what is issued. It is what can be used. When systems are tested, what matters is not what exists in theory, but what remains accessible in practice. Under pressure, identity collapses into function.

# The First Break

The system does not fail all at once, nor in a way you immediately understand. The signals you need to recognize failure are the ones being removed. What you feel first is the impact, not the analysis. Consequence, not recognition.

The assumptions holding infrastructure together—warning systems, access points, coordination—are not constant. They are dependencies. They work only when the environment supports them. When that environment shifts, the system does not collapse in order. It fragments. Some parts continue. Some degrade. Some disappear when you need them most.

Inside that moment, the change feels immediate. Not because everything stops, but because the margin for error disappears. When that margin is gone, delay and failure become indistinguishable.

In both cases, the system is unavailable. You act without it.

Kate Taylor calls that instant a rupture in expectation. Explosions arrive without warning. "All my organs exploded inside me." The missing sirens are not just absent features. They remove the sequence that turns risk into action. When that sequence breaks, the system no longer guides behavior. Behavior takes over.

Most systems assume failure arrives in a manageable way. Warning before impact. Access long enough to use. Degradation is slow enough to adapt. But the first break often reverses that. Consequence precedes signal. Impact precedes interpretation. And the tools meant to manage it are already part of the failure.

That inversion makes the break absolute. Timing is no longer a buffer. Without timing, you cannot use the system as intended. Engagement needs sequence, and sequence needs stability.

Stability is gone. When sirens do sound, they come after. Not as instructions. Confirmation. The thing they warned about has already happened.

Shelters are locked. Proof that the system did not expect this moment. People bypass structure. Cut locks. Find other ways in. Not because they are told to. Because there is no other option. Infrastructure does not fail alone.

Every part is tied to assumptions—availability, timing, coordination. When those break, the system does not degrade evenly. It fractures. Gaps appear that design cannot fill. Behavior fills them. In real time.

Kate's note that there was no panic is not the same as no fear. Panic needs uncertainty plus inaction. That combination disappears. Necessity replaces it.

If the system gives no guidance, you act. Now. Composure is not a choice. There is no time to hesitate. When the system fails, the question is not what should be done. It is what can be done with what is left.

The line between system and person collapses. The system stops directing behavior. People stop waiting. Action comes from what is available in the moment—not what was supposed to be.

Victor Gry's story sits inside the same break—and then goes further. Failure moves past protection into coordination. Communication towers are hit. Channels cut. You lose not just warning, but the ability to organize. The need to coordinate doesn't go away. It increases.

A man calls from under the rubble. The call itself shouldn't work. The network that would normally carry it is already degraded. Still, the signal holds— just long enough. That is enough to start a response. Not through a system working as designed, but through fragments. Carried forward by people.

This is the shift. From system-dependent coordination to behavior-driven coordination. Structure doesn't produce inaction. It forces new pathways. Volunteers organize. Civilians move supplies. Networks form. No central orders. Only necessity. Speed becomes everything. How fast these patches form decides whether the gap can close.

Victor does not describe it as a transition. From the inside, there is no sense of change. Only action. Responsibility moves. The system is no longer the primary mechanism. People become the agents of coordination—not by rebuilding the system, but by making enough of it work under new conditions.

Rebuilding is uneven. Resources are uneven. Information is incomplete. Some responses work.

Others are late. Others never happen. It depends on which fragments still function—and which can be stretched by people.

The insight is simple. Failure does not remove the need for a system. It reveals what was essential and what was not.

When only certain functions return—communication, supply movement, coordination—you see what actually matters for continuity, even in a degraded state. This is where the idea that systems fail slowly breaks.

The failure that counts is not gradual decline. It is the moment of maximum dependence. When you need the system the most—and it cannot respond.

Degradation and collapse merge into one condition: unavailability. That condition forces a shift. From reliance to substitution. From waiting to acting. The system does not disappear. It becomes secondary.

Its value is measured by how quickly it can meet needs.

Anything that cannot operate at that speed drops out. What replaces it is not a system. It is a bundle of behaviors—emergent, improvised—that approximate what was lost. Coordination without central authority. Without full information. Without guaranteed outcomes. Fast enough to keep things moving where the original system could not.

This is the first full break. Not a single point of failure, but a shift in how action begins. The system stops driving. It becomes one input. Human responses take over. Acting overrides the design meant to guide it. The point is not that systems are useless. Their roles change under pressure.

Control gives way to support. Primary becomes secondary. Systems that persist are the ones you can operate directly, extend with effort, and use without waiting for stability. Once the system fails at the moment it matters, the question changes. Not whether it worked as designed, but whether anything can still be used. That difference decides whether the system collapses or continues in a reduced but usable form.

What follows is not a recovery. It is a reorientation around absence. Once the expectation of sequence is gone, it does not return quickly. The behaviors that replace it harden. They become the main path for coordination. Not designed systems—patterns that proved fast enough to matter.

Speed is the only threshold left when consequence compresses time. The assumption that systems provide continuity flips. Continuity comes from repeated behavior—from people doing what others can rely on, even without direction. What emerges is not the old system restored. It is a parallel layer. It runs alongside the fragments that remain. Sometimes it reinforces them. Sometimes it routes around them without delay.

This inversion is not abstract. The system that once mediated coordination cannot keep up. Delays that were acceptable now register as failures. Decisions change. The question is no longer whether a system exists, but whether action can be taken with what is immediately available. Volunteers become coordinators. Civilians move supplies. Informal networks take on functions that were once centralized.

Victor's account continues inside this reorientation. It is not tidy. It is many responses that only resemble a system after they are already in motion. Calls. Messages. Broken signals moving through whatever channels remain. That shows not the persistence of infrastructure, but the persistence of intent.

Coordination does not stop because people act. Even a weak signal—a partial message—is enough to start movement. Under pressure, completeness is not required. Only enough to act. This is where the idea that systems fail slowly breaks down for good. The failure that matters is the instant dependency meets unavailability.

When expectation meets absence, the system is redefined by what it cannot do. Everything that follows works without it. Coordination does not wait. It begins as soon as it can—however it can. Messy. Incomplete. Often clumsy. But it exists. And in that moment, existence matters more than optimization.

Optimization assumes time. Time is gone. Kate's memory of that first night—body reacting before the mind, warning absent, anticipation and reaction collapsing—becomes the baseline.

Once the system fails on the first impact, you stop expecting it to handle the next. Expectation drops. Behavior replaces structure. Not because it is better. Because it is immediate.

I saw the same shift in another form. Systems I thought were stable were conditional. Not guaranteed. Structures that seem solid fail at the moment you rely on them most. That is the gap—between believing in a system and knowing its limits. You only see it under pressure. You only feel it when consequences stop being abstract.

In Ukraine, that gap is lived. The first break becomes the reference for everything that follows. Once people see the system fail when it matters, they stop assuming it will hold again. That loss of assumption changes behavior. Coordination emerges without waiting for validation from structures that have already failed.

What forms is not a replacement system. It is overlap. Responses stacking on each other. Together, they approximate what was lost.

Personal networks rebuild supply chains. Information moves through whatever channels remain. Decisions are made locally and acted on immediately. Distributed coordination is not designed. It is assembled in real time—by necessity, not architecture.

Victor shows how these responses stabilize. Not predictable, but repeatable. Behavior hardens into structure quickly when necessity reinforces it. A route used once gets used again. Repetition creates expectation. Expectation becomes a form of informal reliability—something that functions like infrastructure, even without guarantees.

This does not stop failure. It does not make the outcomes uniform. Resources remain uneven. Information stays incomplete. But it reduces the gap between need and response enough to preserve continuity.

That narrowing decides whether the system has collapsed or continues in a reduced form.

The system does not disappear when it fails. It becomes a layer. One among many. Its authority drops. Its reliability is questioned. But it still matters—where it still works.

People do not abandon it. They adjust reliance. Use it when it is available. Route around it when it is not. The shift is subtle but total. The system becomes something you check in real time—not something you assume.

Marie's line lands differently now: "You never know when things can go south." Not a warning. A condition. Access is unstable by default. Operating without "obligatory trust" is no longer optional. It is required. That pushes behavior toward systems you can use directly—not ones that require permission to function. And her counterpoint holds: "blockchain is not magic." It blocks the search for a silver bullet.

Decentralized systems carry their own dependencies. Their own failure modes. What holds is not a winner. It is a combination. Systems used together—each covering what the others cannot.

Layered identities and coordination become the only workable path under pressure. No single system covers every failure. Movement between systems matters more than trust in any of them.

Resilience does not live inside a system. It emerges from interaction—between systems, and between systems and people using them under pressure. After the first break, the line between failure and function blurs. It is no longer a property of the system. It is a question of whether people can keep acting.

That capacity is uneven. It depends on access. On knowledge. On proximity to resources.

Under pressure, the system's role shifts. It stops trying to direct every action. It enables what it can. It stops controlling outcomes. It supports them where possible. Systems that remain useful are the ones that work within that reduced role—usable quickly, extendable by behavior, trusted conditionally, not absolutely.

Once the first break exposes the limits, everything that follows is filtered through it. Expectation changes. The system is no longer assumed to hold. It is treated as something that might fail. And that shift reshapes behavior—how people interact, how they plan, how they respond, and how they decide if a system is working at all.

The first break is not just experiencing failure. It is recalibration. Reliability stops meaning performance. It becomes useful in the moment. The value of a system is no longer its design, but what it can still do when assumptions fall away.

Once a consequence arrives without warning, and the system cannot bridge the gap between risk and action, one question remains: what can still be used?

Everything that follows builds around that answer. Not what the system was meant to do—but what it still enables.

When the system fails at the moment it is most needed, it stops being the foundation for action. It becomes one option among many. What follows is not a recovery. It is adaptation without permission.

# What Holds / What Adapts

After the first break, systems do not vanish. They separate. Failure does not disperse evenly.

The idea that a system either works or does not breaks down. It becomes granular. Some functions fail immediately. Others continue unchanged or degraded. Sometimes even strengthened by the same conditions that caused failure elsewhere.

Continuity and collapse exist at the same time— often within the same system. It depends on what is being tested and how much that part relied on assumptions that no longer hold. This unevenness decides what holds and what adapts.

Survival is not random. It tracks how much a system can operate without the conditions that are gone. Systems that require coordination, timing, or centralized response break first. Systems that can be run locally, extended through behavior, or executed without delay persist. Not because they are better, but because they depend less on what no longer exists.

Pradeep Goel's work on shelters shows this directly. Infrastructure you assume is universal turns out to be uneven. A shelter you cannot enter is the same as no shelter at all. A space you can use immediately—even if it was not designed for that—becomes infrastructure by meeting need in the moment.

The line between design and function collapses into one test: can it be used when needed? Infrastructure does not fail everywhere at once. Effectiveness depends on how closely it matches real conditions. Systems built around ideal access, controlled entry, and predictable use struggle when those expectations break.

Systems that can be repurposed, accessed without mediation, or adapted in real time are the ones that hold. Not because they are perfect. Because they are available.

The same pattern appears at scale. Complexity is assumed to create fragility. Sometimes it creates resilience.

Organizations that had already distributed operations, separated presence from function, and built continuity into structure can reroute instead of collapse. Work shifts across geographies. People move. Output continues. Not because they are unaffected—but because they have enough flexibility to absorb disruption.

Andrii Vyviurka describes the relocation of thousands of engineers and their families as an extension of an existing capability—not a one-off response. The system does not stop and restart. It continues in a different configuration. Productivity persists under conditions where it should not. Why? Because the system does not depend on a single point of operation. It can move without losing function.

Resilience at scale is not the absence of disruption. It is the ability to reorganize around it. That separates systems that hold from those that fail. Dependence on fixed structures drops. The system bends to conditions instead of forcing conditions to match the design.

That adaptability is practical. You measure it by what continues—work, services, value—despite the environment. New systems appear quickly. Faster than traditional structures can adapt. Not because they are inherently faster, but because they avoid layers of coordination, approval, and validation. They sit closer to need. Decisions are made and acted upon without waiting for alignment across the hierarchy.

Vasylchuk's line captures it: "it took just a few days" to build coordination that links people, organizations, and government into a working network.

Removing friction is risky in stable conditions. Under pressure, it is decisive. Immediacy outweighs the risks of speed. Systems that move fast dominate. Not because they are flawless, but because they are timely. Here, adaptation and emergence blur.

Fast adapters resemble new systems. New systems assemble from old parts. A hybrid layer forms— repurposed fragments stitched into new coordination. The same pattern extends outward. Influence no longer moves only through formal channels.

Digital platforms compress coordination into the information layer. Governments can speak to corporations, to people, and to global networks in real time. Pressure forms immediately. Action follows visibility—not negotiation. Coordination under pressure is not only physical. It is informational.

What ties these cases is not the systems themselves, but their properties. They operate without delay. They extend through behavior. They function without the conditions that have already failed. That is why they hold. They do not wait for recovery. They work under the new conditions.

They are not immune to failure. They degrade. But they provide continuity when it matters. They bridge the gap between the break and whatever comes next—recovery, replacement, or further adaptation.

What holds under pressure is not what was designed for stability. It is what keeps working when stability is gone. What adapts is not what changes slowly, but what reorganizes in the moment—using what remains to create enough structure, enough continuity, enough coordination to prevent total collapse.

Scale, visibility, and resources do not decide survival. The question is simpler: how much can the system run without the assumptions that were invalidated? After the first break, systems that require alignment across many points fall behind. Systems that work locally, immediately, without waiting, persist.

The difference between design and use collapses into one test: can it be accessed when needed?

This is clearest at the physical layer. Infrastructure is not defined by presence. It is defined by usability. A shelter that exists but cannot be entered fails like one that was never built. A space you can access immediately becomes infrastructure because it meets a need. Access is not guaranteed; it is conditional. The line between protection and exposure is whether entry happens without delay.

Infrastructure does not fail everywhere. Its effectiveness tracks how well it fits actual conditions. Systems built on controlled access and predictable patterns struggle when those patterns break. Systems that can be entered without mediation, adapted in real time, or repurposed by users hold. Not because they are better. Because they depend less on what has already failed.

Presence no longer guarantees function. The ability to act without waiting defines what remains usable. But limits remain. Accessibility is uneven. Repurposing depends on awareness and proximity.

Even within systems that hold there are gaps design cannot fix. Resilience at this level is partial, not absolute. Holding versus failing is not a simple either-or. It shifts depending on who can get in and when.

The same pattern shows up in organizations. More complexity should mean more fragility. Sometimes it becomes resilience. Systems that already distributed operations and decoupled location from function bend instead of break. Work shifts. People move. Output continues—not because nothing changed, but because the system can reconfigure while conditions are unstable. It does not wait for calm. It adapts within the chaos.

GlobalLogic shows this at scale. Relocating thousands of engineers and their families was not a pause. It was a continuation. The system did not depend on a single hub, so the output held while the structure changed. Andrii Vyviurka describes it directly: "We moved over five thousand engineers and their families." Not an endpoint. Ongoing change. "Ninety percent of our engineers are productive." Not because disruption disappeared, but because it was absorbed.

That capacity comes from not being tied to specific conditions. Systems that require steady infrastructure, centralized control, and fixed locations break when those disappear. Systems that operate across environments, shift workloads in real time, and avoid single points of failure hold. Not because they are immune. Because they do not depend on any one thing.

Continuity here is not stability. It is reorganization. The same properties repeat. Size and sector matter less than how a system meets its environment. Immediate use. Extension through behavior. Reconfiguration without waiting for alignment. This is not accidental. It answers the same pressure: speed.

Under pressure, delay becomes failure. Survivors run at the speed the environment demands—not the pace that their design assumed. The measure of resilience flips. What holds is not what stays the same. It is what keeps working while changing.

What adapts is not what develops slowly, but what reorganizes in the moment. It uses what remains to keep going. You only see this after something breaks.

The first break removes the conditions that the system expected. It forces immediate action, or the system is left behind. Coordination must change with it. Structures that once organized action become too slow, too dependent. The need to coordinate does not drop. It intensifies. What replaces slow structures is not redesign. It is immediacy. Mechanisms that work at once. No approval chains. No waiting for validation. Completeness is traded for speed.

Vasylchuk's example makes it concrete: "it took just a few days" to build coordination linking people, organizations, and government into a working network. That is not just efficiency. It is friction removed at the moment it would otherwise stop action.

In calm conditions, removing friction looks risky. Under pressure, waiting costs more than imperfection. Systems are not deployed—they are assembled. In real time. From what already exists. Connected by intent, not hierarchy. Extended by participation, not control. Anyone can contribute. At any scale.

As Vasylchuk notes, contributions ranged "from one dollar to one million." Not just inclusivity. Compatibility. Each input connects immediately— without waiting for alignment.

Immediacy separates what adapts from what fails. If action requires coordination first, nothing happens when coordination is the bottleneck. Systems that allow action first—and coordination after—operate within the time window that exists. Execution comes before organization.

That inversion creates tension. Speed reduces oversight. Less friction increases mismatch.

Vasylchuk's line makes sense here: "Bureaucracy killed this program." In stable conditions, bureaucracy provides control. Under pressure, it blocks action. The trade-off is exposed—precision versus immediacy—and the old system cannot resolve it.

Marie's point about removing "obligatory trust" fits here. Fast coordination cannot depend on traditional checks. It must allow participation without prior relationships or institutional approval. Decentralized methods are no longer optional. They become necessary—not because they eliminate risk, but because they enable action when central control cannot.

A new coordination layer forms. It cuts across boundaries. It links people who would not normally work together. Action happens without formal structure. This layer sits between systems—drawing from each, constrained by none.

It does not stay contained. The same traits that allow it to function under pressure extend outward. This is where digital diplomacy appears—not as a separate function, but as a continuation. Direct communication. Immediate response. Real-time pressure. A system under strain influencing others that are not.

You see it in how governments engage companies and global platforms. Not through slow negotiations. Through immediacy, visibility, urgency, and coordination—used to force action that would otherwise take much longer.

Under pressure, influence moves outside formal channels. It travels on the same tools that speed internal coordination. The boundary between inside and outside becomes porous. Speed that organizes internally also enables interaction between systems.

Actions in one place trigger responses in another. Systems link through shared conditions, not prewritten agreements. By now, the pattern is clear. Systems that hold, adapt, and emerge share the same properties. They run without delay, extend through behavior, and do not depend on conditions that have already failed. This holds across infrastructure, organizations, and coordination networks.

At a certain point, these properties stop supporting survival and start reshaping the larger system. One resilient system pressures another to change— through interaction, not design. These systems do not stand alone. They exist in a web of dependencies; all tested at once.

That networked pressure accelerates change. One system's response becomes the condition for another. Acting fast in one place raises expectations elsewhere. Others adapt or fall behind. Therefore, digital diplomacy looks less like persuasion and more like pressure, as immediacy becomes leverage.

Limits remain. Speed does not guarantee accuracy. Reduced control creates fragmentation, overlap, and waste. Systems emerging from this phase are not stable in the old sense. They continue to change and depend on participation.

Resilience is dynamic. It lives in interaction— between systems and people. What holds under pressure is not a fixed design. It is a set of capabilities that can be used across contexts to keep function alive while form shifts.

Once a system is forced to run where delay equals failure, the definition of "working" changes.

Completeness gives way to immediacy. Precision yields to usability. Control turns into participation. Systems that match this definition persist—and spread. The rest fall away, no matter how well they were built for conditions that no longer exist.

This is the shift from failure to continuity. Not rebuilding the old system, but operating within a layered environment—multiple systems coexisting, interacting, covering for one another. Resilience becomes distributed, not centralized. It does not depend on any single system holding. It depends on enough systems running at once to preserve continuity.

What holds under pressure is not what stays unchanged. It is what keeps working while things change. What adapts is not what evolves slowly. It is what reorganizes in the moment—using what remains to create enough structure to act, enough coordination to respond, and enough continuity to persist.

After the break, this is the only measure that matters: what can still be used.

# What Emerges

What emerges under pressure is rarely what would be selected in advance. Not what would pass through layers of design, testing, and approval given the time. It is what can function without those processes.

These systems often appear incomplete or informal when measured against prior standards. Yet they persist. Not because they meet those standards, but because they do not constrain them. They are built at the point of need, deployed quickly, and extended through participation rather than formal processes. Outcomes that would seem improbable under design-based evaluation become possible when judged by use.

Traditional assumptions link scale to coordination, coordination to structure, and structure to time. Under pressure, that sequence reverses. Action precedes coordination. Coordination happens around actions. Structure emerges only where repeated actions create it. In this context, immediacy outweighs alignment—even if alignment would produce greater efficiency.

This shift becomes visible at the individual level. People perform system functions. Not replacing formal structures, but executing roles that those structures would normally mediate. Intent translates directly into action without waiting for authorization. The boundary between participant and system becomes less distinct. Individuals do not just interact with systems; they help make them up.

NFT-based funding illustrates this dynamic. Not because of the technology alone, but because of how it is used. Artists, creators, and participants convert attention into value, and value into action, without institutional intermediation. Max Krupyshev describes this from within the conditions themselves, where creation and response converge.

Execution is embedded in participation rather than organized after it.

The enabling conditions are not new. But under pressure, they become decisive. Tools that allow digital value transfer, decentralized ownership, and permissionless participation move from optional to necessary. Systems that once appeared experimental become primary—not because they are fully matured, but because they operate within the time constraints imposed by the environment.

The contradiction is obvious. What emerges does not resemble formal systems beside it. Yet it performs essential functions for them. Informal, decentralized, often improvised mechanisms operate alongside formal structures—sometimes replacing them, more often filling the gaps those structures cannot close quickly enough.

Context determines everything. As one artist put it, "I am answering from a bomb shelter." Creation and consequence collapse into the same moment. Selling or issuing an NFT links directly to acquiring equipment, supporting people, and sustaining systems that can no longer rely on traditional channels.

The absence of mediation enables this. Steps occur without waiting for validation from external authorities. Contributions move directly into action. When people say "everyone is helping the country as best they can," they are describing a system that has extended beyond its formal boundaries—one that treats participants as active inputs rather than passive donors.

This expansion is neither uniform nor efficient. Openness introduces variation, inconsistency, and friction. Under pressure, those costs are secondary. Immediate action outweighs optimized outcomes. An imperfect system that operates now outperforms an optimal system that arrives too late.

Once the environment no longer supports careful optimization, this trade-off becomes structural. What begins as individual action aggregates. Repetition produces patterns. Patterns create expectation. Expectation forms structure, even without formal design. This is how distributed efforts converge into functional systems.

Coordination emerges from shared purpose and repeated action, not central planning. Initiatives like Art for Life illustrate this dynamic. Artists, groups, and supporters operate as a unified system—not by design, but through necessity. Creation, funding, and distribution align through participation rather than hierarchy, allowing the network to scale without centralized control.

Participants themselves do not always describe this as coordination. It appears as a natural extension of existing behavior. As Peter Ivanov notes, "We collected all our backgrounds and launched this initiative." The defining feature is not structure, but the speed of formation.

Under pressure, speed takes precedence over design. Yet this form of emergence introduces its own tensions. Value becomes both practical and symbolic. Contribution and expression converge. Motivations become less distinct. Participation can signal impact or recognition, often both.

This raises a further question. As these systems expand, can they maintain focus? Can a structure built on immediacy sustain coherence as scale increases? The same openness that enables rapid formation may also introduce drift.

These tensions do not prevent the system from functioning. The underlying mechanism continues to convert participation into action, regardless of individual motivation. Therefore, statements like "crypto is the easiest and fastest way to collect money" appear. They are observations about utility under constraints. In these conditions, speed and access outweigh concerns that would dominate in stable environments.

A similar shift occurs in trust. Without centralized validation, verification moves elsewhere. Not to authority, but to visibility. When institutional guarantees are absent, participants rely on evidence of outcomes. Transparency becomes operational rather than symbolic.

White Rabbit addresses this directly by making verification integral to execution. Transactions, purchases, and deliveries are documented and shared as part of the process. Andrej Šimunaj emphasizes documenting "every single receipt, every detail." Transparency is not an added feature. It is a requirement for continuity. Without centralized validation, the system persists only if outcomes remain visible.

This aligns with the broader pattern. Systems that emerge under pressure share the same properties as those that hold and adapt. They operate without delay. They extend through behavior. They function within the constraints imposed by the environment, even when traditional systems fail.

What distinguishes them is where they originate. They do not emerge from established institutions, but from the gaps those institutions leave when they fail. Their legitimacy derives from performance rather than design. Validation comes from outcomes rather than expectations. Systems that would not meet traditional criteria can still function under pressure.

As a result, those criteria lose relevance. The primary test becomes whether the system can deliver within the required timeframe. Complexity is redefined as usability. Design becomes execution.

These systems don't replace what came before. They reveal what was already possible—but unused. Coordination, funding, and trust can operate without centralized control. Under certain conditions, these approaches are not alternatives; they are necessities.

What follows is not a return to a prior structure, but the addition of new layers. These layers expand the system's reach by introducing multiple pathways for action. The result is more complex, but also more resilient. Systems compensate for one another's limitations.

In this environment, the distinction between system and participant continues to diminish. Individuals do not simply use systems; they shape and extend them through repeated action. The system remains in flux, developing with the conditions that define it.

What becomes clear as these systems emerge is that they are not random. They may appear that way in isolation, but the same traits that determined what held and what adapted continue to shape what follows. Not by design, but out of necessity.

The ability to act without delay. To operate without centralized approval. To grow through participation. These properties recur across layers, whether in infrastructure, organizations, or individual actions. This continuity gives the pattern its coherence.

Emergence is not separate from what came before. It is a response to the same constraints that produced failure, shaped by the same environment, and therefore subject to the same requirements. Under pressure, systems that would not persist in stable conditions can function effectively. The criteria shift. Complexity reduces to usability. Optimization gives way to immediacy.

NFT-based systems formed during the war illustrate this clearly when viewed as part of a pattern rather than as isolated experiments. Their effectiveness does not come from formal structure, but from alignment with conditions. They allow participants to convert attention into resources, resources into action, and action into impact without waiting for traditional coordination layers. Statements like "everyone is helping the country as best they can" reflect this dynamic: a system that extends beyond formal boundaries and incorporates participation at scale.

The limits, however, are equally clear. Speed introduces variability. Participation creates inconsistency. The absence of centralized control increases the risk of fragmentation. These systems are not stable in the traditional sense. They remain adaptive, continuously adjusting to the behavior of participants and the constraints of the environment.

Resilience here is not permanence. It is persistence. That persistence connects these systems to what came before. The same participants move across layers—using decentralized funding while interacting with state identity systems and organizational structures. That overlap binds layers that would otherwise remain separate.

Strengths in one layer compensate for weaknesses in another. This is how continuity survives when no single system can hold alone. Vasylchuk's observation that systems could be created "in just a few days" gains additional meaning here. The same capacity that enables rapid coordination also enables rapid system formation. It extends the response beyond its initial limits.

Under pressure, speed is not an advantage—it is a requirement for participation. Systems that cannot operate at that pace fall out of the response. Design does not compensate. Systems that meet the required speed, even imperfectly, are incorporated.

The result is a layered environment in which multiple systems operate simultaneously, each contributing where it can.

Marie's concept of removing "obligatory trust" remains relevant, but it introduces a further implication. Reduced reliance on central authority shifts responsibility to participants. Engagement becomes active rather than delegated.

Trust becomes something enacted rather than assigned. Users function as contributors to system performance. Each participant becomes a point of execution, extending the system through action rather than waiting for instructions. This distributed function aligns with conditions where centralized control would introduce delay, and delay would cause failure.

What connects these observations is the pattern. Systems that emerge under pressure share common characteristics: they are immediately usable, operate without delay, and expand through participation. These same properties determined what held and what adapted.

Resilience, therefore, is not a property of an individual system. It is a function of the interaction among systems under constraints. Once disruption occurs, the relevant question is no longer which system is optimal, but which systems remain usable. The answer is not singular. It is layered.

Multiple systems operate in parallel, each sustaining continuity within its scope. This layered structure shapes what emerges. It does not replace prior systems; it extends them. New pathways for action, coordination, and trust develop alongside existing ones.

The result is increased complexity, distribution, and adaptability—accompanied by reduced predictability and control. This transition—from centralized structure to distributed capability, from planned systems to emergent ones—marks the shift from response to evolution.

What begins as a response to failure becomes the foundation for what follows. Not by design, but out of necessity. Systems that prove themselves under pressure persist as conditions change, carrying forward the traits that allowed them to function when others could not. Not because they were originally built that way, but because they can be used immediately.

What begins as response becomes structure. Not by design, but out of necessity. Systems that emerge under pressure do not replace what came before. They extend it, reshape it, and redefine what it means for a system to work.

# Old Paradigms Die Hard

Once a system has been defined, broken, adapted, and extended, something else becomes visible. Not just how it behaves under pressure, but the assumptions that shaped it.

Systems do not fail at random. They do not adapt without limits. They follow the logic with which they were built. And when that logic no longer matches reality, the system resists before it changes. It holds onto structures, processes, and definitions that no longer work—not because they are useful, but because they are familiar.

This resistance is not unique to any one system, nor confined to moments of crisis. But under pressure, it becomes unavoidable. The conditions that once made systems appear stable have been removed. What remains exposed is where control resides, how decisions are truly made, and how quickly what felt permanent becomes irrelevant when it cannot keep pace.

The instinct to preserve what exists is not irrational. Systems accumulate. Rules, habits, and expectations layer into continuity. That continuity carries value—but only as long as the system still fits its environment.

When the environment shifts faster than the system can respond, those same layers generate friction. Their slow response, restricted action, and reinforced patterns no longer produce intended outcomes. This is where control and adaptability come into conflict. Systems optimized for control depend on coordination, validation, and sequencing. Each of these requires time.

Under pressure, time disappears. And when it does, the system faces a constraint it cannot resolve through its existing logic. The response shifts toward execution over alignment, toward action without permission, and toward growth through participation rather than direction.

What Ukraine shows is not that one model replaces another. It is that the balance between them shifts with conditions. Systems built for control perform well in stable environments. They provide consistency, predictability, and scale. Under pressure, they struggle to move fast enough. Systems designed for adaptability—often less efficient in calm conditions—prevail because they can respond immediately.

This shift appears across domains. Identity systems must function without delay. Physical infrastructure must be usable without mediation. Organizations must reconfigure in real time. Coordination must occur without centralized hubs. New systems emerge without predefined blueprints.

The pattern is consistent: under pressure, the ability to act outweighs the structures designed to guide action.

And yet, misaligned systems do not disappear when they stop working. They are institutionalized—embedded in policy, regulation, and expectation. These layers persist beyond their usefulness.

Change rarely occurs at the moment of failure. It follows as alternative approaches show effectiveness and existing systems gradually lose authority. "Old paradigms die hard" is not a metaphor. It describes systems that continue because they are familiar, not because they are functional.

Replacing them requires not only new systems but a different understanding of how systems should operate. This pattern is not confined to large-scale crises. It appears wherever stability is assumed rather than validated. Systems that seem reliable reveal themselves as conditional when their environment shifts. When that happens, the cost of misalignment is immediate. It forces a reassessment of what reliability actually means.

This reassessment connects to the broader argument. The builders operating under pressure are not testing theoretical models. They are responding to necessity. Necessity removes abstraction. It reveals which systems remain usable, which assumptions hold, and which structures can adapt in real time.

Leadership changes under these conditions. It shifts from maintaining control to enabling action. The role is less about enforcing process and more about removing constraints. Effective leaders do not direct every outcome. They create conditions that allow others to act, extending the system through participation rather than limiting it through control.

Phrases like "everybody is a hero" are often interpreted as rhetorical. Here, they describe a structural shift. As systems move from centralized control to distributed capability, the distinction between leader and participant diminishes. Contribution becomes leadership. Coordination remains, but it is redefined—focused on alignment of intent and direction, while execution occurs at the edges where response is fastest. Clarity of purpose paired with flexibility in execution.

This pattern extends beyond Ukraine. The pressure there is extreme, but the systems being tested are not unique. Economic, technological, and social forces accelerate everywhere.

That acceleration challenges traditional structures. The digitization of value, the expansion of coordination, and systems that operate without a single center are not isolated developments. They reflect a broader shift in how systems are built and how they behave. They will not displace existing structures overnight, but they are altering the conditions those structures depend on—making adaptation a requirement rather than a choice.

The properties that enabled systems to function under extreme pressure—immediacy, adaptability, and reduced dependence on centralized control—become more relevant as change speeds up. Systems that cannot operate within these constraints become progressively less viable. The transition will not be immediate. Existing systems were designed for different conditions. Adapting them requires more than new technologies. It requires rethinking structure, decision-making, and the distribution of control. Therefore, resistance persists even as the need for change becomes more apparent.

What Ukraine provides is not an ultimate model, but a reference point. It reveals limits and possibilities. It shows what breaks, what holds, what adapts, and what emerges. In doing so, it offers a clearer view of how systems will need to evolve as similar pressures accumulate elsewhere. The question is no longer whether systems will be tested, but how they will respond when they are.

The answer will not come from design alone. It depends on alignment with conditions, the capacity to adapt at speed, and the ability to enable action without unnecessary constraint. When reduced to fundamentals, what remains is not the system as designed, but the system as used—defined by function rather than structure, and by outcome rather than intention.

This distinction will shape what persists. Systems do not endure because they are well-designed. They endure because they remain usable.

The shift carries a second consequence. As systems behave differently under pressure, they are understood differently. Once the assumption of stability is removed, it cannot be fully restored.

When systems fail at the moment they are most needed, trust moves from theory to practice. Passive reliance gives way to active evaluation. Systems are no longer accepted as they are presented; they are tested against what they actually do.

The expectation that a system will hold shifts into an understanding that it might not. The change is gradual, but its effects persist. When people are forced to act without the support they once assumed, they return to those systems differently—even when conditions stabilize.

The deeper shift is not confined to systems themselves. It changes the relationship between systems and the people who use them. Control moves away from fixed structures toward access. Participation moves away from permission toward capability.

This is visible in how builders operate. Sergey Vasylchuk's observation that coordination could be created "in just a few days" reflects more than speed. It lowers the threshold for participation. It reduces barriers. It compresses the distance between intent and action. Structure follows execution rather than preceding it.

Marie's point about removing "obligatory trust" extends this further. Compressed coordination does not eliminate risk; it redistributes it. Individuals evaluate systems in real time, deciding which to rely on and which to ignore. Decentralization does not produce disorder. It produces a unique form of order—one shaped by behavior rather than design.

That behavioral layer determines whether systems persist beyond the moment of crisis. Infrastructure can be rebuilt. Organizations can be reorganized. But shifts in habit, expectation, and assumption endure. When they change, systems must adjust or become irrelevant. Pressure to evolve comes as much from participants as from formal redesign.

Systems define what people can do, but people also redefine what systems are expected to provide. A feedback loop forms. Each reshapes the other. Stability depends not only on structure but on whether participants can and will sustain function.

Within this loop, the boundary between system and participant continues to erode. Individuals take on roles of execution, validation, and coordination. They operate as components of the system itself— not as extensions of centralized authority, but as distributed points of capability. Therefore, phrases like "everybody is a hero" carry structural meaning. They describe a system that depends on widespread participation to function.

Distribution of capability remains uneven. Hierarchy does not disappear; it is reconfigured. Leadership shifts away from direct control toward enabling action. The emphasis moves from dictating execution to aligning intent. This allows the system to extend beyond any single structure.

When centralized control can no longer keep pace with conditions, distribution becomes necessary. Systems that persist are those that allow control to disperse without losing coherence—maintaining enough alignment to function and enough flexibility to adapt.

What makes this shift matter beyond the immediate case is that the conditions exposing it are not unique. Their intensity may be unusual, but the underlying forces are widespread.

Technological, economic, and social changes are accelerating. As they do, the gap between design and reality widens. Systems operate under increasing pressure, and the same patterns recur across contexts. Delay becomes a failure.

Centralization becomes constraint. Adaptability determines whether systems continue to function.

The digitization of value, the distribution of coordination, and systems that operate without a single center are not fresh developments. What is new is their convergence. Together, they amplify one another, reshaping how systems are built and how they are used. Acting quickly becomes essential. Independent operation becomes viable. Growth through participation becomes more effective than centralized control.

Centralized systems do not disappear. They continue to provide capabilities that distributed systems cannot fully replace—coordination at scale, regulatory alignment, long-term stability. But the balance shifts. Distributed systems assume roles that centralized systems struggle to perform, particularly where speed and flexibility are required.

Systems don't survive because they were built to last. They survive because people keep them alive. Through use, through adaptation, and when necessary, by working around them. What endures is not the design. It's the capability to act.

What Ukraine shows is not replacement, but coexistence. Multiple systems operate in parallel. Each contributes. Each has limitations. The result is a layered environment in which resilience emerges from interaction rather than dominance. Systems compensate for one another. When one fails, others sustain continuity. The structure is complex and uneven—and it works.

This layered configuration reduces dependence on any single system. It creates multiple pathways for action. When one pathway is disrupted, others remain available. Continuity persists even as conditions change.

Resilience, in this context, is not the prevention of failure. It is the prevention of collapse. Yet this introduces new challenges. Interactions among systems become less predictable. The absence of centralized control can produce conflict, duplication, and inefficiency. Governance must adapt—balancing flexibility with sufficient coherence to maintain function.

Old paradigms resist this shift. They were designed for control, stability, and predictability. Changing them requires more than new technology. It alters how decisions are made, how authority is defined, and how systems are evaluated. As a result, the transition is gradual.

Existing systems persist even as their limitations become clear. Persistence, however, is not the same as relevance. Systems that cannot adapt lose significance—not through formal replacement, but through disuse. People and organizations adopt alternatives that better align with their conditions.

The systems that are actually used become the systems that matter.

This pattern repeats across layers—identity, infrastructure, coordination, and emergence. The shift is not abrupt. It is a rebalancing. Traits that enable systems to function under pressure become increasingly important, even in stable conditions. They shape how systems are designed, operated, and evaluated.

The central question is no longer whether systems will change, but whether they will change in time. Alignment with the environment determines persistence. And that alignment depends not only on system design, but on the people who build and use them.

This gives the shift its significance. It is not confined to moments of crisis. It reveals how systems behave when pushed beyond their assumptions—exposing both their limits and their potential.

What persists is not what was designed to last. It is what people continue to use. Systems endure only as long as they remain aligned with reality—and reality does not wait.

# About the Author

Jamil Hasan is the founder of Crypto Hipster Publications and host of the Crypto Hipster Podcast, a platform built around a single idea: where builders talk freedom, not price.

Across over 580 conversations, he has focused on founders, entrepreneurs, and independent creators—the people actively building the digital economy from the ground up. His work does not center on market cycles or short-term narratives, but on the motivations, risks, and convictions shaping new systems.

His approach is rooted in separating the signal from the noise. In an industry often driven by speculation and surface-level commentary, he prioritizes long-term thinking, first-principles discussion, and authentic perspectives.

Before fully committing to the digital asset space, Jamil built his career across financial services and data-driven initiatives, including work connected to blockchain, artificial intelligence, and client-facing strategy. That foundation informs his ability to translate complex technological change into clear, human insights.

After stepping away during a period of intensive medical treatment, he returned with a sharper lens and a more defined mission: to elevate real builders, reject noise disguised as insight, and focus only on what endures.

*Builders Under Fire* reflects that mission in its most direct form—capturing how systems and the people who build them are tested, reshaped, and redefined under pressure.

# Crypto Hipster Conversations

A list of podcasts that form the basis of this book is presented below, in order of appearance in this book. All of them can be found at the Crypto Hipster Podcast station wherever enjoy your favorite podcasts. Dates of publication are as published on the Crypto Hipster podcast channel and are followed by the original conversation dates.

- CBDCs, Digital Transformation, and the Aid for Ukraine Initiative, with Sergey Vasylchuk at Everstake (August 8, 2022; March 22, 2022)

- Helping Ukraine Refugees NOW with White Rabbit NFTs, Andrej Šimunaj (August 9, 2022; April 15, 2022)

- Attaining Personal Freedom with a Decentralized Identity and Blockchain Technology (Marie Poteriaieva) (August 6, 2022; February 7, 2022)

- The Fight for Sanity and Freedom, and the Revolution of Dignity - a Ukrainian mother

and artist's story of Courage (Kate Taylor)
(August 1, 2022; May 18, 2022)

- S.O.S. WAR IN UKRAINE, Kiev needs help,
Victor Gry (August 4, 2022; March 2, 2022)

- Creating Shelters on the Frontlines of
Ukraine's Border Crisis (Pradeep Goel) (July
27, 2022; February 20, 2022)

- Helping Fund Ukraine with Crypto Worms,
Andrii Vyviurka (August 4, 2022; March 15,
2022)

- Unifying global businesses, fending off global
terrorism, and the future of Ukraine, Max
Krupyshev, CoinsPaid (August 8, 2022;
March 5, 2022)

- Rebuilding Communities with Ukraine's
ArtforLife NFT Campaign, Peter Ivanov
(August 9, 2022; April 6, 2022)

www.ingramcontent.com/pod-product-compliance
Lightning Source LLC
Chambersburg PA
CBHW021326060726
47591CB00006B/1896